Eli Shepperd's

Plantation Songs

Introduction by
Barbara Hardaway, Ph.D.

Edited by
Pia Seija Seagrave, Ph.D.

Sergeant Kirkland's
Fredericksburg, Virginia

Published & Distributed by

Sergeant Kirkland's Museum
and Historical Society, Inc.

912 Lafayette Blvd., Fredericksburg, Virginia 22401-5617
Tel. (540) 899-5565; Fax: (540) 899-7643
E-mail: Civil-War@msn.com

Manufactured in the USA

The paper in this book meets the guidelines for permanence and durability
of the Committee on Production Guidelines for Book Longevity of the
Council on Library Resources, Inc.

Library of Congress Cataloging-in-Publication Data

Shepperd, Eli, [pseud]. Young, Martha, 1868.
  [Plantation songs]
  Eli Shepperd's Plantation Songs / Introduction by Barbara Hardaway,
Ph.D.; edited by Pia Seija Seagrave, Ph.D.
        p.   cm.
  Originally published: Plantation songs. 1901.
  Includes bibliographical references (p.)
  ISBN 1-887901-11-6 (alk. paper)

1. Plantation life – Southern States – Poetry. 2. Afro-Americans – Southern States –
Songs and Music – Texts. 3. Afro-Americans – Southern States – Folklore – Poetry. I.
Seagrave, Pia Seija, 1952- , II. Title.

PS3547.05P5   1997
811'.52—dc21

                                    97-9670
                                    CIP
                                    AC
                        First Edition
        1 2 3 4 5 6 7 8 9 10

Cover design and page layout
by Ronald R. Seagrave

EDITOR'S NOTES

Eli Shepperd's (Martha Young) *Plantation Songs*, in its rarity and compelling drama, is a book that cried out for republication. The spirit of the songs, the wonder of the photographs, and the story they weave of plantation experience combine to render this volume a remarkable find in the world of Southern history. For us at Sergeant Kirkland's, it has also been somewhat of a detective story, as we sought and found the true identity of the author/compiler, and as we continue to look for and collect information on the life and writings of Martha Young.

Eli Shepperd was born Martha Young, near Greensboro, Alabama, the daughter of Dr. Elisha and Ann Aliza Ashe (Tutulier) Young, just three years after the close of the American Civil War, in 1868. As a child, she grew up during reconstruction in the South.

At age thirty, Martha Young attempted to publish and promote her first title, *A Tale of the Spanish Invasion of Alabama* under her own name, and found it to be a man's world.[1] In 1901, she published, under the name Eli Shepperd, her 1901 work entitled *Plantation Songs*, with a sub-title *For my Lady's Banjo....* She made her home in Greensboro, Alabama, and never married.

Barbara Hardaway, my esteemed colleague at Gallaudet University, graciously consented to add her expertise in the introduction to this work. Ron Seagrave has assisted in the artistic lay-out, design, and formatting of the text and photographs, as well as the design of the cover. I have changed very little of the book, preferring to let the words and melodies and visual representations of this slice of plantation life

---

[1] We have located only one copy.

speak for themselves. While I am sensitive to comments about the inclusion of potentially offensive terms in the text of the songs, I am also committed to the preservation of the original in its full integrity, even as such terms clearly demonstrate the nature of the people's oppressive experience.

We hope our readers will find this volume as moving as we did. Certainly this demonstration of sorrow and mourning, vitality and joy, despair tempered by hope, and the richness of life lived by the people portrayed within these pages merits the preservation and re-telling our publication of this book affords.

Pia Seija Seagrave, Ph.D.
September 1997
Fredericksburg, VA

Martha Young wrote:

A Tale of the Spanish Invasion of Alabama. s.l., Martha Young, 1898.

Plantation Songs: For My Lady's Banjo, and other Negro Lyrics & Monologues / by Eli Shepperd [pseud]; with pictures from life by J.W. Otts. New York: R. H. Russell, 1901.[2]

Plantation Bird Legends / by Eli Shepperd [pseud]; with illustrations by J. M. Conde. New York: R. H. Russell, 1902. New York: D. Appleton, 2nd ed., 1916. Freeport, NY, Books for Libraries Press, 1971, ISBN: 0836987780.

Bessie Bell. New York: s.n., 1907, 2nd ed.

Somebody's Little Girl. New York: Hinds, Noble & Eldredge, 1910.

Behind the Dark Pines, with illustrations by J. M. Conde. 1912. Freeport, NY: Books for Libraries Press, 1972, ISBN: 0836991338.

When We Were Wee: Tales of the Ten Grandchildren. New York: Macmillan, 1913. 2nd printing, 1914.

Two Young Southern Sisters and Their Garden Plays. New York; Philadelphia: Hinds, Hayden & Eldredge, Inc., 1919.

Minute Dramas, The Kodak at the Quarter. Montgomery, AL: The Paragon Press, 1921.

She also published the following songs:

Sweet Shrub
Mammy's Sleepy Song
Minute Dramas
Kodak at the Quarter, 1921.

---

[2] In the past fifty years, McGrath's *Bookman's Price Index* reports only one offering of this title for sale, (see vol. 25, 1983). In 1997, noted antiquarian bookseller, Robert Douglas Sanders / McGowan Book Company, Durham, North Carolina, reported having only a single copy, several years ago. We have located only four copies of this text, at Brown University, George Mason University, Sergeant Kirkland's Museum & Historical Society, and North Carolina Central University Library. The Library of Congress had no reference for this title.

INTRODUCTION
by
Barbara Hardaway, Ph.D.

This collection of musical folklore, monologues, love ballads and spirituals is a testament to the oral traditions of African-Americans at the turn of the century in rural America. The songs are a lyrical mosaic of themes that move along a continuum of tender love ballads to commentaries of the harsh realities of human bondage and social degradation. The language and the central themes reveal irony, levity, and a vitality that create a literary tradition of wit and bittersweet humor. In this antebellum narrative genre, the dialect is often in poetic verse, lyrical, bold and rich with imagery that brings to the reader the cultural spirit, imagination, and social conditions of its people.

African storytelling traditions came to the shores of the North American continent in the early 1600s with the arrival of the first enslaved Africans. The Slave Period lasted until 1865 and was the era which furnished the literary background for the entire framework of the Negro folklore idiom. Of African origins, these songs were influenced by social inequality in this country, historical experiences in the rural South and European folklore. The context of these plantation songs reveal multicultural influences that express overlapping literary and musical contributions from Africa, Europe, and North America. Notwithstanding, the narrative and musical traditions that have evolved in this country are unique expressions of a time and of a kidnapped African people who sang and danced and cried and laughed at

themselves and at America in order to survive human bondage and abject poverty that was passed down from one gen-
eration to the next. Many of these plantation songs were cre-
ated out of sorrow and cruelty as expressed in the stanza
about "Ole Elam."

> "Ole Massa's kilt at Cedar Run,
> Ole Misses' days is long been done
> Eh! long as dem two was alive,
> Dey need ole Elam, sah, to drive.
> Ole Massa'd hit dat man- ho-he!
> Dat'd call Elam's room better 'n his company!"

These songs of melancholy and vitality that echo the
voices and sentiments of an oppressed people are also tales
of celebration and hope. The plantation songs also make up
a lampooning genre with their fanciful plots and jocular
vigor that express enduring hope and are full of promise.
This is seen most vividly in the humorous courtship rituals
of the persistent suitor, Job, who serenades his Roxanne into
long-awaited romantic bliss. We find that love and determi-
nation do, indeed, reign supreme in melodies from "Songs
for My Lady's Banjo."

> "Surely no strings can happier be
> Than those she touches frequently:
> So, pretty banjo, do your best,
> Follow her lightest, sweet behest,
> Right merrily!"

We have in Eli Shepperd's collection of plantation songs
a slice of musical, oral tradition whose roots are ancient, in
tales and songs that provide us with invaluable insight into
the lives and thoughts of thousands who were once America's chattel.

The songs presented are more than a body of entertaining stories for the reader's amusement. They open the door into the oral records of a people whose humble lives reveal the irony inherent in the New World's concepts of slavery and freedom. This storytelling, musical tradition further provides insights and a special appreciation for this type of secular and religious folk expression. Black folk tales and songs were first recorded in the late nineteenth century. Contemporaries of this early period, interested in preserving folk expression, used phonetic dialect as a literary device, feeling that an exaggerated colloquial language best expressed the attitudes and lifestyles of southern Blacks of this era.

The most popular instrument of choice for plantation songs was, typically, the banjo. Of African origins, the early "banjos" were first made by African slaves and are based on original percussionist instruments with strings that were plucked like a harp. These drum and gourd-like prototypes continue to be played in parts of West Africa today. The popularity of banjo music spread rapidly during the pre- and post-Civil War years throughout this country despite the initial disapproval and disdain it received from the more affluent members of American society. Regardless of the well-to-do classes' impression that the banjo was fit only for lower-class people within communities that engaged in exaggerated jig-dancing, the banjo was enthusiastically appreciated by the majority and became a favorite of millions by the turn of the century. This versatile musical instrument was played on southern plantations, in Civil War battlefields, and on minstrelay stages. Eventually, the banjo even found its way into the parlors of the affluent as a classical style of performance developed and as continued improvements and changes were made in the instrument. The banjo, indigenous to the African continent, remains part of America's proud musical tradition today and is a keeper of people's voices and hopes.

Pictures by J. W. Otts emerge from the lyrical and sentimental verses of the songs and depict rural scenes and do-
mestic family life on the plantation. They provide us with
classical images of the people, their circumstances and the
times in which they lived. In several of his portrait pieces,
Otts has captured a range of emotional expressions that echo
the mood and literary messages of the verses; they provide a
visual context for the written words. The complimentary re-
lationship between the passages and visual images is made
most apparent with "Roxann, the belle of six plantations" in
the banjo series and is reflected in other passages as well.

Shepperd's collection of plantation songs highlight experiences and relationships among people in the late 1800s.
The songs chronicle events such as the end of the Civil War,
the raising of the "Yankee flag" at the "Great House," and the
surrender of the wounded "Marster. " Uncle Aaron's lyrical
description expresses passion and conflict in his acknowl-
edgment of the plantation's surrender and desire for a uni-
fied America.

"Well, come and le's go 'long and see
If dey is done surrender or not
Maybe Marster done give up de place
Widout even parley or shot. "

Cultural and historical information imparted to the
reader includes knowledge of seasonal tasks, holidays, and
ways in which the African-Americans prepared for "hog
killing times, white Christmas, Green Fust of April, and
Bright Fo't' of July" while in servitude on southern plantations. Animal songs and folk tales about Brer Lizzard, Sis'
Mole and Brer Buzzard are designed to teach lessons and
cultural values while providing entertainment with their
levity and humorous rhymes. Time and time again, we find,
throughout this collection, that creativity, laughter, and tears
kept the plantation folk alive and gave them strength to sur-

vive in poverty and with the many injustices that were inherent to plantation living.

Through these plantation songs, hymns, and stories, we are able to revisit our American past and can pay tribute to a literary folk tradition from a people who were denied their human rights to be educated in this country. Despite these many injustices, and perhaps even because of them, plantation songs and stories remain alive today. Their significance lies in the preservation of a people's culture that bondage and poverty could not destroy. The plantation song genre is a dialectical adventure of yesteryear that embodies humorous narrative, Old and New World folklore, and American history. It not only amuses and befuddles the reader, but provides applied folk knowledge, religious strength, and wisdom that sustained the souls of its people and lifted their voices to sing.

Barbara Hardaway, Ph.D.
September 1997
Washington, DC

Plantation Songs

Plantation Songs

FOR MY LADY'S BANJO

And Other Negro Lyrics & Monologues

By ELI SHEPPERD

With Pictures from Life by J. W. OTTS

NEW YORK · R. H. RUSSELL
PUBLISHER · *Nineteen Hundred and One*

UNIVERSITY PRESS . JOHN WILSON
AND SON · CAMBRIDGE, U. S. A.

To my Father

WHO WAS ONE OF THE NOBLEST TYPES OF THE OLD SOUTH, AND
WHO BORE FORCEFUL PART WITH THE HEROIC
UPBUILDERS OF THE NEW

Table of Contents

Hymns of the Black Belt

TABLE OF CONTENTS

Plantation Songs

Songs for My Lady's Banjo

TAKE you this tinkling instrument,
   Strung up with gay and mad intent,
Strum it with dainty finger-tips —
It is a jester full of quips —
   This gay banjo.

To the most sentimental sigh
With tittering tones it will reply,
And only laughter need expect
The answer that it would elect
   From this banjo.

'T is not a thing for serenades
Beneath the windows of fair maids:
No whit cares it for vows or tears;
It cuts sighs short — a pair of shears —
   This bright banjo.

Yet to the maid of Africa,
The ebon maid of Zanzibar,
Its twanging measures might suggest
Love thoughts she'd deem the tenderest —
  Her swain's banjo.

For hear the dusky lover sing,
Shooting his fancies on the wing,
An improvised, absurd love-song;
He fits it as he goes along
  To his banjo.

L AS' dance gwine dance to-night
 Down in Holly's gyarden;
My gal, yo' eye so bright —
 I wisht my heart would harden!

Las' light de moon gwine give —
 She wiltin' now, I see;
My eye's like a sieve,
 Sift you through and through me.

Las' song gwine sing to-night
 Down in Holly's gyarden;
O gal, yo' hair so bright
 I sho' hit slick wid lardin'.

SONGS FOR MY LADY'S BANJO

My gal, she 's des as black
    Ez airy lily's shadder —
So light fer airy fac'
    She float up Jacob's ladder !

Miss Ladies, cyard and spin,
    Down in Holly's gyarden ;
Miss Pretties, lemme in
    To watch you at dat cyardin'.

My gal, yo' mouf so round
    No black-berry rounder —
And den yo' teef so sound,
    Nairy pepple sounder.

Oh, my ! yo' eye so bright,
    Down in Holly's gyarden,
Hit gwine cyarve my heart outright, —
    And never ax my pardon !

PIANO, harp, and psaltery
    Take for their rôle : Grand Melody,
And the guitar and violin
Play for their part : Sweet Heroine.

In music's drama as they play
Our hearts with noble passions sway : —
Banjo must be Jack Pudding here,
Appearing but to disappear ;
But we 'll remember that the fool
Is often Shakespeare's sharpest tool.
So : true Hans Wurst, this same banjo
Will have his say before he 'll go ;
No reverence he for court or king,
Before the judge's door he 'll sing
His parodies upon the law ;
In strongest proofs he 'll pick a flaw,
Through longest briefs his nonsense draw ;
Will witness what he never saw !
But since good-nature is so free,
For once to listen we 'll agree,
While some dark singer puts to tune
The trial that he had last June :

G EMPLEUM of de Jury, de Likewise, An' —
Ef I stole de pot dén who stole de pan?
Mister Distric' 'Torney 'scuse me of a pig ;
Now who gwine say ef hit little or big?

Oh, Mister Gempleum, please lemme go !
Us better give de pig some time to grow ;
'Caze de bigger is de pig den de bigger is de case,
And de credit to de lawyer dat 's de winner of de race.
Solemn truf, Gempleum, whar de hog 's raise,
Right dar 's de ve'y place whar he gwine to graze.

Now, don't hol' de hog, Jedge, des let him scoot —
He 'll find de ve'y place where he useter root.
Ef he go to *my* house dat 's whar he b'long —
(Wisht I had a stick fer ter drive him along)
Ef, on de contrary, he belongst to *you* —
Le's take him to de country, — and have a Barbecue !

Gempleum of the Jury, de Likewise, An' —
Is you gwine to shut up bof de hog and de man ?
O Massa Jedge, I would n' ef I was you —
Bof 'll be de healthier fer stayin' in de dew !

A H, no respect for Church or State —
That Banjo is insatiate.
Such swelling joy its cheeks inflate,
And so much nonsense doth it prate,

Sure "quips and cranks" upon it wait,
And laughter is its proper mate.
But only blacks in " Open Fiel's "
Will sing for us rollicking " reels " —
For any one who 's "Gethered In "
Will say it is a wretched sin
" To was'e so much dis worl's good win'
Fillin' a banjo's no count skin ;
And worser yet hit 's al 'a 's been
To lend yo' voice sech reels to spin ! "
All lively sounds but make up grist
For Brer Dig's grim, dim mill of Mist.
His arguments the singers end
With laughter at their good old friend,
With hitting faults they cannot mend, —
For faults always with fixtures blend.
See ! the gay rhymer shuts his eyes,
Throws back his head and sings thus wise :

OLE Brer Hawk in de Amen Cornder,
Jaw in his claw he sit and ponder ;
Rain-crow he 's a high-head member, —
Jine de band sence las' December.

Thrush he belong to de Singing Choir,
Callin' de Seeker : Higher ! Higher !
'Pecker-wood pass his hat around,
Keep his eye sot on de ground.

Yonder 's de cat-bird rockin', rockin',
Rockin' 'long wid a hole in her stockin' !
Ole Brer Buzzard hollerin', shriekin',
Singin' : Glory ! and de Preacher speakin'.

De Mournin'-Dove des deep in mournin',
And dat Whip-Po'-Will cyarn't cease groanin' —
O my Brothers ! Please come th'oo !
Yas ! My Brothers ! Beg you do !

GOOD this banjo with five tight strings,
King Instrument at " Puncheon Flings,"
Where all the colored damsels walk
Down a slim line that's made with chalk ;
And three dark judges must decide
Which walks with most ease, grace, and pride.
Now see young Rox Ann take the floor
(Surely no duchess could do more),
Her shoes, home tanned with red-oak bark,

At every step they " squeak and squawk " :
" Dem what beats her dey got to walk ! "
Then Job takes up his tuned banjo,
To make an interlude, you know,
Consents to sing a song or two —
" Dat round de Ole-Time Song-Tree grew."

Miss Katy at de cake-walk —
    Move des so !
Corn-tossle on de stalk
    Swing des so !
O make a pretty motion, — tu-re-lu-re!
I got a mighty notion, — tu-re-lu-re !
    Who gwine take
     De cake!

Mosquito say de Katy-did ma' y'd her cousin,
    Cousin, oh !
Mosquito keep up sech a mighty buzzin',
    Cousin, oh !
Katy-did say : Katy did ! Katy did n't ! Dee ! dee !
Locust holler : Come see ! Come see ! See
    Who gwine take
     De cake.

*M*AKE *a pretty motion — tu-re-lu-re —*
I got a mighty notion — tu-re-lu-re —
Who gwine take de cake !

Oh, Miss Jincy, pigeon-toe,
                    Move des so!
Backin' same as de crawfish go,
                    Creep des so!
Dem whar gits hit gits dere potion, — tu-re-lu-re!
Dem whar gits hit: Land er Goshen! — tu-re-lu-re!
                    Who gwine take
                              De cake!

THEN the crude minstrel, pressed for more,
     Draws out from his melodious store
A summer song of birds and bees,
A song that's set young maids to please:

O SUMMER-BEE in de willer tree,
     Please, sah, fill-a one comb for me;
But all dat honey in dat Souf
Is not s' sweet as Mandy's mouf!

O clover-patch, behine yo' latch
De sweetes' flowers grow and match;
Dey are not so pretty, dat I know,
As my Mandy.   I 'll tell her so!

PLANTATION SONGS

O sugar-cane, you 're ripe again,
As full er juice as clouds er rain ;
But, oh, dem tears in Mandy's eyes
Air sweeter when she sof'ly cries !

Dem thistle-seed, folks name 'em weed,
Air swift to foller breezes lead :
But I turn quicker on my track
When Mandy calls me to come back !

BUT when daylight begins to creep
  Across the earth that 's half asleep,
" Ole Day 'gins move his white-wash brush,
And does his business in a rush ! "
Frolickers know their time is up,
" De pretty walker 's got de cup ! "
Then in a spirit of abandon
Job gives the banjo to old Shandon,
And that old rogue will make confession
How certain goods in his possession
Came to him by a " crooked arm,"
(A " crooked-arm " man watch-dogs can't harm).
Ah, hear the thievish fellow sing !
True to his words the banjo 'll ring :

*B*UT *I turn quicker on my track*
  When Mandy calls me to come back —

O PHARAOH!
'Way down in Egypt land,
Gwine tell ole Pharaoh's band —
Let dem people go!
Nigger in de woods settin' on a log,
Let dem people go!
Hand on de trigger, and de eye on de hog,
Let dem people go!
Oh, some folks say dat de nigger won't steal,
Let dem people go!
Ole Master cotch eleven in his corn-fiel' —
Let dem people go!
Nigger is a-pickin' in de cotton-patch,
Let dem people go!
Keepin' all de cotton dat his pockets catch,
Let dem people go!
Nigger is a-slippin' on de 'tater-fiel' —
Let dem people go!
Oh, dat 'possum wid sugar in 's heel!
Let dem people go!
Nigger steal a picayune to buy him a wife,
Let dem people go!
You may save all yo' days, but you cyarn't save yo' life —
Let dem people go!

23

Nigger set a trap in de highes' grass,
Let dem people go!
If it cotch Misses' turkey it 'll hol' him fas' —
Let dem people go!
O Pharaoh!
'Way down in Egypt land,
Gwine tell ole Pharaoh's band
Let dem people go!

THEN as the crowd breaks up to go
Job takes again his own banjo,
And, walking close behind Rox Ann,
Makes love to her — ambitious man!
For she 's the belle of six plantations,
Filling men's hearts with sore vexations.
But Job will hope while there is life —
Persistency 's won many a wife!
So through the fields where cotton grows,
Striped by the corn in even rows,
The dusky lovers take their way
Beneath the gray wings of New Day.
They pass great cotton-woods whose leaves
Clap like glad hands; pass the low eaves

ROX ANN:
  She is the belle of six plantations,
  Filling men's hearts with sore vexations.

Of some bare lonely cabin home,
Across the new-plowed, sooty loam ;
Down the white road whose limestone bluff
Is gay with " nigger-heads " of buff ;
Where vines of wild potato blooms
Hang down the banks, drooped, snowy plumes,
White melilotus fills the air
With perfume aromatic, rare ;
And thousand bees are hovering o'er
Those blossoms rich with crystal store
Of honeys sweet as those that fill
The flowers of Hymettus Hill ;
Across the bridges 'neath which gleam
The ripples of the bored-well's stream :
Afar, anear — the pleasant splash,
Artesian waters' downward dash —
A million fountains whose clear gush
Makes Alabama's Black Belt lush.
The morning star still shines apace
Ere the broad sun lifts up his face ;
The hedges are astir with birds ;
Afar they hear the lowing herds ;
The eternal prairie breezes blow
The purple hazes to and fro ;
The morning-glories round the corn

Open their blue eyes to the morn.
Oh, what an hour is this to tell
A damsel that you love her well.
'T is very plain that Job thinks so,
For hear ! he strikes his gay banjo !

D AR 's one flower by de brook
    Dat's got my sweetheart's darkly look
Dar 's des one flower black as she,
And dat 's de ve'y one for me —

O you sweet-shrub,
Dark as my lub !

A many a bloom 's as white as snow,
And many a yaller one I know ;
Des one 's as brown as Roxy's cheek —
Hit grows along Bogue Chitty Creek —

Sweet-shrub ! Sweet-shrub !
O lub ! O lub !

De harder dat you press dat bloom,
De gooder gits hit's good perfume ;
Yit nothin' 'bout dat flower 's gran',
Hit only suit de po' black man.

O dat sweet-shrub,
Black as my lub !

O honey my lub, de grave is green,
O honey my lub, grass is between
De heart dat I would hol' to mine,
And des true heart dat's al'a's dine:

Good-bye, sweet-shrub!

Good-bye, my lub!

Dar's flowers pink, and red, and blue,
Left in de world fer next year's dew:
Dey all may suit some y'o'her eye,
Dey all des make me moan and cry:

Fer you, sweet-shrub!

Fer you, my lub!

NO, Rox Ann is not moved to tears,
No sadness to her heart inheres:
She laughs as gaily as before,
While Job will still his love-talk pour
Into her ear as on they go,
Timing his talk to his banjo:
"Say, why 'n' you marry me? Hum? Haw?
I works—" "Yas! works yo' jaw!"
"I'm name a good hand, dat you know—"
"A good hand on dat ole banjo!"

"Come, Rox Ann, what's de cause to tarry?
I sho' I good enough to marry,
I good —" "Good as ole Harry!"
"Rox Ann I'm pretty now, I know!"
"Pretty ugly! dat you is, fer sho'
And mo''n dat pretty apt to stay so!"
"I got a hoss and buggy, — dat's sho'!"
"Is yo' stable down in Hideyo?"
"Yit I suits yo' and yo' suits me —"
"Young ox go *Wo* when you tell him *Gee!*"
"But I love you and you must love me —"
"Shoo! all dese niggers is set free!"
So gay Rox Ann goes on her way,
Leaving her lover in dismay —
He to turn brave face to defeat,
Will join the jay in carol meet
To show he will not deign to be
Despairing for such maid as she:

DAR, Miss Nigger! Hard to please!
 Gwine de lef' fer de winter breeze —
Same like corn-stalk lef' in de fiel',
Lef' fer de nex' year's wagon-wheel!
Go 'long, Nigger, I don't keer,
Somebody 'll hab me, don't you fear!

" *GOOD* hand on dat ole banjo ! "

SONGS FOR MY LADY'S BANJO

YET scarce the clock one hour can mark,
 Scarcely has day thrown off the dark,
Ere Job feels that he's been too rough,
Quite ready he to cry : Enough !
And Rox Ann, too, begins to sorrow —
All youth is quick of grief to borrow.
Great fear she feels that she will lose
The lover that her heart would choose,
Three buckets for her load she goes
Where the artesian water flows ;
She puts one bucket 'neath the stream
And stands enwrapped in half a dream.
Job has filled up the food-troughs now,
And has drawn out his double-plow, —
On the plow-beam he takes his seat
To wait until " de mules done eat."
Together he and his banjo
Utter the saddest notes they know —
The song old Elam often sung
Before great silence touched his tongue :

I SETS on dese heah rottin' logs,
 I watch dis drove of pigs and hogs,
I drives 'em off from ev'y gap

Dey find in Mister's sorghum-crap —
   Dem hogs dey grunt an' dey says to me:
     Elam's room 's better 'n his company!

I sets beside de kitchen fire,
De blazes runs up high and higher,
De darkeys laugh and joke around,
Dey call ole Elam's room: " Was'e Groun': "
   Dey ruther have, I easy kin see,
     Ole Elam's room dan his company.

Ole Massa 's kilt at Cedar Run,
Ole Missis' days is long been done —
Eh! long as dem two was alive,
Dey *need* ole Elam, sah, to drive.
   Ole Massa 'd hit dat man — ho-he!
     Dat 'd call Elam's room better 'n his company!

Missis could n't do widout me, — Dar!
I 'bleeged to drive dat skittish pa'r —
Dat Dick and Dolly 'd run 't was plain
Onless ole Elam helt de rein!
   But now so no count Elam be
     His room 's wof mo' 'n his company!

I SETS on dese heah rottin' logs —

SONGS FOR MY LADY'S BANJO

THE limpid stream has filled the pails,
    And Rox Ann lifts them by the bails,
One on her head, one in each hand,
She steps across the dew-wet land,
And — strange — her road lies just that way
Round which the banjo's tinklings stray.
(In all love's lore this axiom 's true :
The Long Way Round Is The Short Way Through !)
She walks with stately step and slow,
She passes Job and his banjo :
Then she sends back her even voice
In words that make Job's heart rejoice :

WATCH out, Nigger man, what you 'bout,
    You 'll sholy wear dat banjo out —
            Let 'lone dis gal !

I 'll tell you what I 'll hatter do —
I 'll be obleeged to marry you,
            And dat I shall.

I bound to make yo' big mouf hush,
And knock dat banjo inter mush
            Befo' I die !

37

I mus' give dem po' strings a pause,
I 'll marry you fer des dat cause
        And reason why.

⊙⊙⊙⊙⊙⊙⊙⊙⊙⊙⊙⊙⊙⊙

A ND so you like this gay banjo ? —
    It little suits a hand of snow ;
Yet still on Music's Sea 't will float
A pretty, skimming pleasure-boat,
        Right merrily !

Among the ships upon Sound's Sea
(A sparkling sea of Harmony)
'T will ever drift a lively craft,
While gayest breezes round it waft,
        Right cheerily !

Forever down its good taut strings
Laughter will murmur light nothings ;
In truth we could not well dispense
With this meek friend of no pretence —
        Nay, verily !

Then little banjo, ever float
On Melody, a jolly mote, —

THREE buckets for her load she goes —

SONGS FOR MY LADY'S BANJO

Touched by my Lady's finger-tips,
And sung to by her dainty lips,
      Right cheerily !

Surely no strings can happier be
Than those she touches frequently ;
So, pretty banjo, do your best,
Follow her lightest, sweet behest,
      Right merrily !

Uncle Aaron's Greeting : A Monologue

At the Quarter

WHAT! Come back from Santiago?
　　And wearin' his arm in a sling —
Lawsy marcy, ole 'oman, heah dat!
　　Don't dat beat ev'ything?
Take my hat off de peg, Jerushy,
　　I ain't had it down for a year ;
Git my long-tail-black, out de chist dar
　　You!　Handle dat coat wid keer :
My folks wore dat coat th'oo three sessions —
　　Ole master, his pa, and his son —
You has to have 'spec' for a coat
　　That 's been th'oo de years like dis one.
Hu! yu! Den.　I 'm stiff in the jints,
　　But walkin' 'll limber me some.
Git my cane out de cornder, Jerushy ;
　　Now call dem boys : Lewis! oh, Lum!
Come go wid gran-pa to de Gre't House —
　　And come quick, you lazy young coons ;
Yo' marse Tom is come from de wars
　　Des tetotally kivered wid woun's !

42

UNCLE AARON'S GREETING

I feel sorter now like a gen'leman,
    Dar's virtoo in dis coat, I believe,
To make me feel most like a scholard
    Wid de larnin' dat ole master leave
Des hangin' around in dese pockets,
    Or maybe slipped up in de sleeve.
I feel now as spry as a sojer
    Off a day on a bravery leave.

Singing

Dar's blood on de clouds and de moon's shickle 's sharp,
De angel is strikin' war-chunes on de harp —
For he's struck his shickle in de harves'-fiel',
And a many a soul has to crouch and creel;
For he'll gether de grain in his gol'en hand,
And a many feet 'll press on de gol'en strand —
    Yes! my brother! you oughter been dar
    When de winds blew free and far!
    O! my sister! You oughter been along
    When de death-wind swept so strong!

Dem winds air filt wid breath of de dyin'
(Dyin' breaf sets de winds' wings flyin').
O! my brother, de angel was dar
When de woun's fell nigh and fell far:

When de cradle was struck in de fiel'
When War turned de chariot-wheel —
    Yes! Dat wheel is fleein' and flyin',
    Whirled by de sobbin' and de sighin'!
    Swift wid breaf of so many a dyin',
    Sobbin' wid cryin' and sighin'!

On the Path

Hold up, chil'en, de ole man 'bleeged to rest.
    Lemme set on dis log des a spell,
I must wait twel my strengt' rises some'at —
    Good you cotch me — I mos' might er fell!
How quiet de fiel's and de country,
    As still as de ole gin in June.
Dis a cur'us war anyhow,
    Our war wa'n't played to dis tune!
Des Marse Tom, and some one or two mo',
    Few several gone to de fight —
Marcy! in *our* war my master
    And four hunderd 'listed one night!
Ev'y one had his several hosses,
    Nigger cook, nigger boy, nigger man;
Besides from dis ve'y plantation
    Mos' a whole endurin' brass ban'.
And us melt and roll into bullets

Ev'y teapot and plantation bell,
And us took ev'y plow off de stock
When later us needed mo' shell.
And all day de ladies picked lint,
A-singin' to keep back de tears,
And de quarter-folks tried to raise corn
Wid a passel o' scrubby ole steers,
'Caze our hosses all gone to de front,
And our mules gone pullin' de guns,
And dar war'n't a white man to be seen —
To de front!   All — fathers and sons!
Well, times is obleeged to change,
And de ole ways is mos' wo' out:
Young folks, and new ways, and new wars —
Wonder what dis new war is about:
Never heard of no Spaniards in my time,
De Lord must have made 'em sence.
In Cuba?   Freein' mo' niggers?
Dar 's enough on dis side of de fence.
A passel of skittish free darkeys
As won't let ole folks teach 'em sense.
Well, chil'en, le 's move on along;
De House ain't much fudder, I know,
But, law! when de years git heavy
How long de short paths grow.

Singing

> I 'm on de road,
> I 'm on de road,
> I got no time to tarry !
> I got no load,
> I got no load,
> I got no load to carry !

I 'm on de heaven-road.   I 've los' de sinner's load,
I feel salvation's goad, drivin' me on de road !

> My feet are shod,
> My feet are shod,
> I wear de shoes of John !
> De way he trod,
> De way he trod
> Leads me so gently on !

I 'm on de heaven way, I cannot stop nor stay,
The Leader's voice I will obey, and keep right in de
   heaven way !

At the Great House

   Marcy me ! what 's dat on de tower ?
      Yankee-flag, des sho as I 'm born !
   Heah, chil'en, slip down and hide
      Right heah in dis ruslin' high corn —

"IS my boy beab got on de Blue — ? "

UNCLE AARON'S GREETING

Dem Yankees sure found dat Marse Tom
    Was des come home for a spell,
And dey done come and took dat boy
    Ter deir Dry 'Tugas Prison, or hell!
Dey done raise deir flag on de house!
    Gracious me! what is dey gone done?
I 'spec' neither man nor mouse
    Is left — not nary a one!

Is you crept up and tuck a nigh look, Lum?
    Des tell de ole man what you see —
Ole Marse and ole Miss on de gallery,
    As easy as easy can be?
Den tell me : *Is* dat flag a flyin'
    What I think dat I think I see?
Yas.   And, Lewis, you say dat Marse Tom
    Is come out on de front porch, too?
Is you tryin' to fool yer grand-daddy,
    Or tellin' him truf fer true?
Well, come and le's go 'long and see
    If dey is done surrender or not —
Maybe Marster done give up de place
    Widout even parley or shot.

Lord, boy! Lord, chile! Lord, honey —
    Our boy wid his arm in a sling —

Didn' I teach you to ride! You! sonny —
   Didn' I bait yo' fust hook? Ev'y thing —
And to think you done been to de wars!
   Yit dese arms kin clasp you once mo'.
Bless de Lord for dis day, little massa!
   Dis day — He-he! ho-ho! ،
My soul, boy — De brass and de buttons —
   Sojer-straps! — and des one heavy fight?
But — What's dis I see? Gracious me!
   Tell me — oh, does my ole eyes see right?
Is my boy heah got on de blue?
   Shoo — den — oh! I scarcely kin ax it—
Is you 'serted and left us for true?
   Don't you know dem gray cloze in de chist
In camphire laid up in de lof'?
   Don't you know how us cried when us fold 'em?
Even Marse hid a sob wid a cough.
   Come heah! boy! Tell me! — what you done?
Is I done load yo' very fust musket,
   Fer you ter be feared of a gun?

Hu! You laughin' at dis ole nigger?
   Des tell me, den, what all dis mean,
Fer dat flag and dese cloze is de beatenes'
   Things my old eyes even seen.

UNCLE AARON'S GREETING

You say that you follered Joe Wheeler
　To de rifle-pits down at Caney?
Dat's right.　Us follered dat Wheeler
　From Tupelo to Kintuck — like you say.
And you say Wheeler rallied 'em on
　And won de whole glorious day!
Now, boy, dat talkin' sounds good
　In de good ole-fashioned way.
But you say he rallied his men
　Round *dat* flag, and led men from New York?
I sholy believe my senses
　Gwine ac' like a mustang — and balk.
And us all des one country now,
　Same as had no Great War at all?
Call it de "late onpleasantness" —
　Gone like first frost in de fall —
Hu! boy!　Time changes and changes,
　Changes may be for better and all,
But you can't 'spec' a stupid ole nigger
　Ter stretch his mind round de whole ball.
All I know is: With things gwine like you say
　Den us nigh to de golden sho',
Whar dey eats des butter and honey,
　And whar Yankees ain't Yankees no mo'.

April Rhymes and Rigmaroles.

HEAR Uncle Roger as he sings
    Of old-time, half-forgotten things,
Of happy times now passed away —
Of foolery for All Fools' Day.
Melodious, clear his old voice rings,
Gay in his poverty he sings:
And all his songs will still display
The negro then as now, — alway
Happy-go-lucky as to-day:

HOWCOME de fools have a 'special day
    And de wise men dey have none?
Dat must be des a laps th'oo'd in
   When de stint of time was done.

Fer de clock run round in a jokin' way,
   And de clouds play tricks on de sun —
De hours seem to have des a minute to stay —
   Des step in to see de fun!

*H*EAR Uncle Roger as he sings
  Of old-time, half-forgotten things —

APRIL RHYMES AND RIGMAROLES

Us kin knock all day at de Great House door,
 Den run round de cornder quick !
Dar 's a holiday fer ev'y nigger on de place
 And nairy a one is sick.

 Aunt Ziny puts cotton in de muffins den,
  And de sugar bowl 's filt wid salt,
De whole plantation gwine on mad
 And nobody callin' halt !

Us kin hitch up an ox to de great big carr'ag'
 Wid a fishin'-pole for a whip —
Us kin play any joke on de Great House folk
 And nobody care a tip !

Oh, de Fools' Day sho' is a jobly day
 And a day to walk wid pleasure,
I 'm sho' hit 's a day like des th'oo'd ın
 Fer to give us extra measure.

De year is awful pleasin' anyhow : dar 's as many colors to
hit as dar was to Joseph's coat. White Christmas, Green
Fust of April, Bright Fo't' of July, and a Brown Michael-
mas-time fer to eat a goose fer to bring good luck fer all
de year round.

Hit's true ef de fools have one whole day
  Dat ev'y man has one,
When he pay de dues somehow, some way,
  Dat he owes to fool and fun !

Des see how Brer Lizzard played de fool
  When he buyed so many coats —
And de mockin'-bird he showed less sense
  When he sign up all de birds' notes !

Sis' Katy-did sho' went and los' her wit
  When she start her Katy did !
Dey cross 'zamin' her a ever sence
  Twel she say : Katy did n't instid !

How 'bout Sis' Mole when she git so proud
  Dat she could n't walk *on* de groun' ?
Fer to show how she done play de fool
  She was put way *down, down, down !*

Brer Buzzard, too, see him walk so proud on a hill-top
some sunshiny day and you 'll think he is wiser dan anybody — yit look how he done ! Laugh at all de nests hung
out for all de birds to try, and hisse'f would n't choose none.
And see him now : when de rain comes he sits drawn up on
a rail fence and croaks out :

A UNT *ZINY puts cotton in de muffins den*
    And de sugar bowl's filt wid salt —

APRIL RHYMES AND RIGMAROLES

" I 'm gwine to buil' me a house in de mornin' !
I 'm gwine to buil' me a house in de mornin' ! "

But de nex' day he 's out in de sunshine as foolish as ever,
— he flies in de highest sky, and he say :

   " Dis is better 'n any house !
   Dis is better 'n any house ! "

IF ev'ybody and ev'ything, I say
 Would des be silly one single day —
Den I reckon de wise folks might and may
Never find nothin' mo' to say —
 But we 'd all des laugh together.

But now hit 's up, and now hit 's down,
Dis one giggle and dat one frown,
One gwine straight, and y' o'her gwine round,
Yet all find de way to Silly Town —
 But nobody laugh together.

If we 'd all choose de day when de Spring is bright,
When de rain and de sunshine don't know quite
Whicherone is de mostest light ;
When de sunbeam 's yaller and de raindrop 's white
 And all des laugh together,

Den de rest of de year we 'd all be wise
And ev'ybody's wit 'ud be one size,
And nobody 't all would be surprise
To see wise folks in a fool's disguise
   Des one day all together!

Brer Lizzard he' fuse to laugh wid de rest of de world, so
de ole folks say, and dar ain't no kinder tellin' now when
he gwine to be tuck wid de wo'se sorter spell of gigglement.
If he meet anybody gwine 'long de big road or de neighbor
path he 'll tuck his head down and laugh, and laugh, twel
he make you feel right foolish fer even des a varmint to
laugh at you so hearty. Mo' 'n dat ef he bite you, you
will get to be a all-de-year-round giggler des like he is.

D AR 'S a heap of fool things gwine on all de year,
    Dat is de truf!
Hit 'd 'stonish folks if folks could hear —
    Dat is de truf!
Now dis heah quar'l 'twixt de kittle and de pot
    Dat is de truf!
Which is de blackest and which is not —
    Dat is de truf!
And de same sorter 'sputement is began,
    Dat is de truf!

*D*EN I reckon de wise folks might and may
  Never find nothin' t' all to say
    But we'd des all laugh together !

APRIL RHYMES AND RIGMAROLES

'Twixt de skillit-lid and de fryin'-pan —
>> Dat is de truf!
And all dis talk 'twixt de pot-hook and de crane
>> Dat is de truf!
Hit 'll go so far dat dey can't explain —
>> Dat is de truf!
Des as silly is de spider arguin' wid de hoe
>> Dat is de truf!
Dey *all* is black!   Don't you think so?
>> Dat is de truf!

But de mos' silly chile of all is de chile dat takes up de fire-stick to scratch de soot off de chimney-back, fer dat 's a sign to bring a whippin' to dat chile sho' — dat is one of de ole folks' signs, dat is.

D EN come along, niggers, play yo' pranks to-day,
>> Den get to work to-morrow —
Des patch ole jokes in de ole time way,
>> Forget wearied lines and sorrow.

'T won't do no harm to unhinge a gate,
>> Or to write a funny letter,
Or to tell Uncle Jake dat de stable 's a-fire —
>> And quickly tell him better!

Send ole Miss a bunch of dog-wood blooms,
    Wid a string of fish tied in it;
Send Marse a log fum de las' bee-tree,
    And he won't find words ag'in it!

Put Limber Jo dancin' on de puncheon-flo' —
    And loosen a plank in de middle —
De way dat nigger'll trip on dat plank
    Will nigh 'bout bust de fiddle!

Set ole Bob playin' wid 's fiddle in 's hands
    And slily grease his bow —
Ask Tuss to strike up a banjo tune —
    Fill de skin wid cotton — Oh! ho!

Oh, dar 's many a way to have much fun
    And never do no harm,
And an all-day laugh is better luck
    Dan airy conjure-charm!

Much as I do b'lieve in de ole folks' signs, I sho' do b'lieve dat a real good laugh is better luck dan even red-peppers hangin' from de jist of de cabin, or sunflowers growin' at de gate, or cotton-cards crossed over de bed-head, and almost as good as a horse-shoe nailed ends up against de do'-facin'.

SET Jo Bob playin' wid his fiddle in his hands,
  And slyly grease his bow —

APRIL RHYMES AND RIGMAROLES

OH, spin me out dat extra day
    Sun flyin' round so high !
I 'm sho' de sun is a spinnin'-wheel
    Spinnin' round dat sky !

Watch de April showers how dey slip up now
    And break off de shine of de day,
Same as chillen round de ole folks' wheel,
    Break off de thread dat way !

Oh, de shine is better for de small rain-fall
    Des so de wind don't blow —
And de Spring of de year is a happy time
    If fros' don't fall no mo' !

Ground-hog ain't feared of his shadder now
    De yaller jessamine 's blowin' !
And ev'y gal is plantin' slips
    To see if her beau's love 's growin' !

De cotton is planted in de light of de moon,
    To do its 'bove-ground bollin' —
De brown branch holes are full of fish —
    And de long fern leaves unrollin' !

Truf, too, de ole folks' signs is all out fer ter tell de chilly season done passed. De beans are sowed in de light of de moon; de root-crops sowed in de dark of de moon, are takin' strong holt in de ground. De flyin'-ants are out in swarms.

SO joke on, niggers, who gwine keer?
　　Us 'll have a good time on de 'vances of de year,
Times is change sence niggers is free,
But he still love to laugh, and dat I see —
Us 'll mortgage up de mule, and de calf, and de cow —
And get out of payin' some way how!
So heah is Buck, Lambskin, and Zo, —
'Tain't de fust time you been mortgage befo'!
Wid a crop-lien heah, and a rent-note dar
Nigger won't hatter hoe his row too far —
And whatever happen at de end of de year
Nigger happy to-day and to-morrow don't keer!
Den in fer de frolic and de fun to-day
No matter what he promise, nigger don't hatter pay —
Nigger have a easy time ever whichaway —
Nigger love little work — and ve'y much play!

APRIL RHYMES AND RIGMAROLES

AH, this old Roger knows his race
    And very rightly states their case:
Never a thought of coming morrow,
Never a sigh for last day's sorrow
Never a moment's look ahead,
Never a tear for grief that's sped.
For such gay hearts an April Day
Sets old jokes out in new array ;
So let them laugh and laugh away
All of the live-long All Fools' Day !

Hog-Killin' Times in Dixie Land

A SUNSET cold, and clear, and red,
   A flock of black-birds overhead,
A crisping chill in all the air —
Sure Jack Frost whispers : 'Have a care!
Ere morning comes you folks will see
A wreath of white on every tree !
The geese send out a creaking call,
The flock of guineas huddling squall, —
While fifty pigs in lot and pen
Run squealing, pushing round old Ben.
Full of sweet corn, and wheat and mast,
They little think to-day their last.
Old Master steps upon the porch ;
The darkeys hasten to approach.
Each hopes to hear : " To-morrow, Ben,
We'll clear out all that squealing pen ! "
What jubilee those words would send
Through all the place from hill to bend.
From out of every cabin door,
From quarter, crib, and field they pour,
Each darkey's face spread in a grin,
" Hog-killin'-times is come ag'in ! "

*O*LE Uncle Dew, *better git out yo' shawl,*
   Ha! Unc' Dew, fer de fros' gwine fall.

HOG-KILLIN' TIMES IN DIXIE LAND

The jolliest time of all the year, —
Hard work, high feed, and lusty cheer !
Old master calls : " Come up here, Dew !
Sometimes yo' nigger-signs come true."
Lo, bent with weight of ninety years,
Old Dew in front the crowd appears :
Then hear his lore of " rats in walls,"
And " frosts sho' falls when guineas squalls,"
When " sheeps stand close, and hosses neigh,"
When " chickens roost ere close of day,"
When " birds come early to their bough."
He don't know when, or where, or how
He learned the signs he utters forth
Of chilling blasts to blow from North.
But e'en this wisdom can't command
Reverence from yonder grinning hand."
Behind the crib hear Dazzle sing,
The while he " cuts the pigeon-wing " :

UNC' Dew know when de fros' gwine fall !
    Unc' Dew hear dem guineàs squall,
Ole Uncle Dew, better git out yo' shawl,
Ha ! Unc' Dew, fer de fros' gwine fall !

73

Fros' put sugar in de punkin'-shell!
Fros' make de 'simmon tas'e so well!
Fros' make de shoats all squeal and yell, —
Oh, la! Honey!   De fros' done fell!

Sugar in de gourd and can't git it out,
Dazzle will ef you let him shout —
String up de gourd, and he may, and he mought
Ring dat sugar in music out!

Hi-ho! Jincy! now for jowl!
For pig-foot jelly a-shakin' in de bowl!
Yonder Berkshire, watch him roll!
Dat pig wof' his weight in gol'!

Oh, la! Massa when de pigs be kill
Who gwine turn dat sausage-mill?
Oh, la! Mistis!   Dazzle will
If you des give spare-ribs to his fill!

BUT now old Dew hints best to wait —
He " ain't seed no snow-birds of late,"
Also " he ain't begin to feel
Dat tetch er fros'-bite in his heel."
The Master thinks a bit, then: " No,
We won't kill hogs to-morrow, Jo!"

*O*LD *Duncan's King in killin' times.*

Then on all faces such a gloom
Falls as this were most direful doom —
Dazzle can dance and sing no more,
The sad news spreads from door to door:
" Ole Massa say we ain't gwine kill, —
Ef us don't to-morrow us never will."
Each " hand " goes slowly to his work,
With more than half a will to shirk.

But down the east a crisper blow
Comes to make bare limbs creak and sough,
Comes to sweep clean the winter sky:
The smoke lines stretch up straight and high,
And that keen sparkle in the air
Bespeaks a frost heavy and fair.

Hear! from the Great House winds the horn:
" Massa done change sho' as you born!"
Cries Dazzle gaily from the pen
Where he's been toting slops with Ben.
From every cabin now they run,
Forty good " hands " if there is one!
Here they come tumbling one and all
To hear the Overseer call:
" Come! Git to work! We're goin' to kill!
Git to it now!   Work with a will!"
But see Old Duncan comes apace,

Pushing among the crowd a place —
Old Duncan 's King hog-killin' time !
That season Duncan's work is prime !

Massa, ready ? Well den ! You, Reason, you hitch up
de young oxen to de ole cyart, go 'long to de fur swamp
whar you, and me, and Marse Charlie, cut dat daid pine-
tree a year ago to git dat fat 'possum, — hit 's *lightwood !*
Haul up ev'y knot of hit. You, Reuben ! run down to de
ten-acre past'er and git up Dancer and Duke. Hitch up
de wagin, and go fetch up a three-thirds load of hickory-
bark fum de new-ground clearin' by river-bend. 'Tain't
nothin' 'll hold fire like bark. Boys, go to choppin' on de
cord-wood ! Whar de chile-minder ? Yond' she ! Aunt
Ailsey, set all de chillen to pickin' up chips 'ginst mornin'.
Us gotter clean mos' a thousand pound of meat on dat
flatform to-morrow. Dar ! I hear de ax-swing and de
song-sing now :

OH, de cedar tree is a mighty fine tree,
   Fer hit grow so tall and hit grow so free !
But she feel my ax-blade belt her round,
Den she come down level wid de ground —
     Wid de ground !
     Wid de ground !

WHAR de chile-minder? Yond' she. Aunt Ailsey,
set all de chillen to pickin' up chips 'ginst tomorrer —

HOG-KILLIN' TIMES IN DIXIE LAND

A notch out de dog-wood! What you 'bout!
You grow so thick and you stand so stout,
But when my ax go whick! go whack!
Den Mister Dog-wood's on his back —
Go whick! Go whack!
Go whick! Go whack!

I'm mighty sorry dem niggers got a dog-wood to cut for de hog-killin'; dat ain't de tree to cut for jobly times like dis. You, Toby, how many plow-shares in de side-shed? Fetch out all de ole iron. Set fire to de log-pile. Stick in de ole iron. Let 'em git red-hot 'ginst mornin'. You, boys! Is you got dat hogshead buried in de ground? Dat sho' is a big barrel, but it ain't too big! Give it a slant on de off-side. Dat's it! Nobody can beat Duncan at de hog-killin'! Fill de pots wid water. Let all be bilin' time day break. I hear dem boys at de cord-wood at dere singin' ag'in:

OH! a ring dis year, and a ring las' year!
And a ring all time for de oak-tree heah!
But when my ax go ring-a-cling!
Den all her rings away she fling!
Cling-a-ling!
Ring-a-cling!

Oh, de beech say de pigs eat all er de mast,
De beech say dey greedy, dey eat so fas';
But now, Mister Beech-tree, you can burn,
Fer every one can have his turn:
    Den le's burn —
    Pig to a turn!

AND now the wagon comes with pine,
    And now the pots are set in line;
The platform stands out new and white;
The log-heaps burn with cheery light.
At every open cabin-door,
Out which the ruddy fire-lights pour,
Some old crone sits and scrubs a pot
For cooking melts, chitlin's, — what not!
Ah, the good cheer to-morrow'll bring
Is fit e'en for Dahomy's King!
Yet each old crone will tell a story
Of better times and greater glory,
For e'en old days looked back to better —
And old folks' tales are ne'er lost letter.
A little rest, a little sleep,
Then soon as Sol begins to peep

DEY are at de ax swing and de song sing now —

HOG-KILLIN' TIMES IN DIXIE LAND

Athrough the rosying eastern sky
Slumber has fled from every eye.
Out of the doors Old Duncan's call
Brings from the cabins great and small.
The pigs are no more pets to swill
From trough and pail their greedy fill, —
They 're now but pounds of pork to kill,
Food for the block and sausage-mill.
Old Duncan orders all about
With loud command and lusty shout.

Empty dem bilin' pots inter dat hogshead buried half in de ground yonder. Hot 'nough? Now. Bring up dem red-hot plow-shares. Shove one in de barrel. Hear how de water sing! Dis is de best time to kill meat, des 'fo' Christmas, — meat is sweeter kilt den. Also we must kill in de *dark* of de moon so dat de meat will wax in de sto'-room and in de kitchen as de moon wax. Ef meat is kill in de *light* of de moon it will wane as de moon wane, it will swink in de pot as hit 's cookin'. Water hot 'nough? Yas. Bring up de hog! Fust kill' to-day! Wonder what he weigh. Dash him in de barrel! Fling him on de flatform! Begin de cleanin' — Now, boys! start yo' song:

PLANTATION SONGS

WHOLE hog or none is de word I sing!
Come 'long, niggers, 'nudder one bring, —
A whole hog! a half hog! a no hog at all!
'Less us have a white fros' early in de fall!

A fat side, a lean side, a no side at all!
'Less hog and hominy sets in 'de hall!
Come, niggers, fetch in de shakin'-jelly-bowl!
Streaks er lean, streaks er fat down de hog-jowl.

Sage in de gyarden, pig in de pen,
Dry yo' sage in summer time, — and Oh, la! den,
A hog fer ev'y growed hand, a hog fer ev'y chile!
Dat make de winter seem very light and mil'!

Oh, de ham meat hit's sweet meat, de bes' meat of all.
Massa mind de kitchen whilst you eat in de hall —
Leave me de back-bone, dough hit be small:
Save me de back-bone or save me none at all!

My massa raise me on hog and hominy —
Dat howcome I likely and jobly, as you see!
Now massa turn de raisin' o'er to me —
He sets me to raisin' hog and hominy!

Bring up anudder hog! Mo' hot iron heah! I see de
womens got dere pots out a'ready. Lawsy! Yonder

EVERY old crone sets a pot —

HOG-KILLIN' TIMES IN DIXIE LAND

Aunt Joanna come down from de Great House to be head taster. Um-hum! 'T ain't often Aunt Joanna 'll mix wid us fiel'-niggers! De chillen a'ready beggin' fer pig-tails to roast in de ashes! White chillen, black chillen, all beggin' fer hog-bladders fer to make balloons. Whoop up, niggers!

THE day goes on with maddening whir,
    It's kill, and cut, and grind, and stir,
Ailsey, and Judy, Locket, Lu,
Critty, and Creecy, Nicy, too,
Have taken each a pot or pan
To stew sweet-breads; while old Aunt Ann
Cooks brains, or kidneys, or an ear, —
Rich odors wafting far or near,
Of liver fried or chitlin's broiled,
Or roasting chines, or pig-foot boiled,
Or crackling-bread upon the hoe —
How rich and brown the steaming dough!
Others are making scrapple, souse, —
Oh! this the round year's best carouse!
E'en Christmas coming on apace,
With Twelfth Night, New Year in the race,
Will find it hard ado to beat —

"Hog-killin' times, so rich, so neat!"
And to hear Dazzle gaily sing
Of the rich things those seasons bring:

D E turkey good, de turkey fat,
    And ole Brer' Possum fatter!
But tell me, Honey, what can tas'e
    Like pig-foot fried in batter!

Dat Pickin' time 's a very good time,
    And Ginnin' time is better!
But if any time 's good as hog-killin' time —
    Why! des send me a letter!

When Christmas comes de eatin 's good,
    Wid egg-nogg in de bowl, oh!
But whar can you find dat eatin' rich
    As a streaked slice er jowl, oh!

A Johnny-cake 's a very good cake,
    'Special roast in ashes!
But what so good as cracklin' bread
    When de bread-hoe fires and flashes!

HOG-KILLIN' TIMES IN DIXIE LAND

Oh, Christmas time is a jobly time,
   And " Christmas Gif' " is jolly —
But a red-hot stchew of marrow-chine
   Is good enough for Holly !

And New Year is a happy time
   Ef de sides are down in salt, oh !
But ef you find no time as good as dis time —
   Why ! you can't find any fault, oh !

Oh, de whole hog rich, and de whole hog fine !
   But kill, and cut, and cure him !
Dar 's sausage, lard, and ribs, and chine —
   Twel you hardly can endure him !

SO goes the busy jolly day
   Till skies are red, then gold, then gray,
The porkers hang all ghostly white,
Strung on a line in the dark night,
Each on its whittled gambrel-stick,
Each one so weighty, smooth, and slick.
Duncan and Frank beside a pot
Of coffee, rich, golden, and hot,
Are set to watch the night go by

To see that no harm comes anigh
The fatted wealth that dangles high.
As Duncan stirs the rosy ashes
From which "roast 'tater" odor flashes,
He sings an old plantation song,
Rolling the jolly notes along :

RINKTUM! rinktum! rinktum! ro!
What's de sweetest root dat grow!
De yam, I say! Do you say so?
Brer' Possum say he do not know!
　　Oh, ho! Yo! ho!

Rinktum! rinktum! rinktum! ro!
Des roast it in de ashes, — so!
And watch how far its good smell go,
Den eat 'em up! Good potato!
　　Oh, ho! Yo! ho!

Rinktum! rinktum! rinktum! ro!
Us watch all night. Us sleep? Oh, no!
Us eat de roast potato, — so!
Don't mind de cole, so wind don't blow!
　　Oh, ho! Yo! ho!

HOG-KILLIN' TIMES IN DIXIE LAND

SO the hog-killin' time is o'er,
   A jovial time in days of yore!
Its homely glory all is fled,
Its jollity named with the dead—
Lost with the things of long ago.
We fit ourselves to new time, — though
The olden days we ne'er forget.
Ah, *tempora mutantur, et*
Nos mutamur in illis. True, —
So we may love both Old and New.

The Passing of Mammy

"YOU say that Mammy is dying?
My dear old Mammy Jo!
Why did n't you come for me, Rosser,
Ever so long ago?
Come, Jubal, saddle my pony
And bring her round quick to the block.
You say she is in your cabin
Away beyond Blue Rock.
Have you been very good to her, Rosser?
She's your only mother, you know.
I wish she had stayed here with us —
So, Jeanie, so, pony, so-o-o-o-o —
Now start on, Rosser, and ride
Ahead just to show us the road.
Here are all the good things in the basket;
That's right, a pretty good load."

How fresh the Spring air in the Maytime,
How pungently sweet the pines —
How golden the millions and millions
Of bells on the jessamine-vines.

THE cabin away beyond Blue Rock.

Ah, there in the dusky cabin,
With the smouldering " chunks " on the hearth,
Reached the dark old arms that had clasped her,
Loved, tended, and held her from birth.

" You, Babsey, — you l'il' gal ! You Petsey !
You is done come to Mam' Jo !
De niggers all say you would n't,
I tole 'em you would : Des so !
Di'n't you useter leave yo' Ma
When I 'd call you to come ? — ho-ho !
Dat useter make Mistis mos' cry
To see how you 'd come when I 'd call —
' I do b'lieve de chile love you, Jo,
Mo' 'n me and her Pa, and all !'
Oh, Honey, de ole times is banished,
Gone whar de ole times go,
Us don't know whar dey be vanished,
Des know dey don't come no mo'.
You sorry I lef' you all, li'l' Miss ?
Well — I gwine lef' *dem* all now —
Co's Rosser was des a nigger,
But den he was mine, anyhow.
Dis cough — No'm — No doctor — No money —
But don't you fret 'bout dat, chile,

God's will cyarn't be stopped no way, Honey,
And us all bound to go somewhile.

" I sont fer you now, li'l' Lady
(I done miss you so all dese years),
Fer to ax you to meet me in Glory, —
I gwine miss you dar, too, I fears,
Dis black preacher heah to Swamp Church
He says no white pusson cyarn't go
Nairy bit way furder in Heaven
Dan de ve'y outermos' do'.
But I 'm gwine ax de Good Master
To — ' Please, Sah ! ' — des let *you* in !
'Case I don't wanter go 'long feruvver
Missin' you so ag'in.
I know you cyarn't have much 'ligion
'Caze you ain't never had no chance,
But de Lord won't be hard on you, Honey,
When I tell him des way things advance —
You al'a's had so much er money,
And no trouble to draw you nigh
(Who ? — my ole Massa's Gran'chile ;
Troubles 'bleeged to pass her by !),
And you al'a's had gracious plenty
Of mighty good things to eat.

M*AMMY and de Baby Chile.*

THE PASSING OF MAMMY

Naw! you don't know how quick, my darlin',
Honger 'll draw you right down to God's feet.
Some mornin's, when I does so miss
My sugar and coffee *or* tea,
I hatter wrestle in prayer some hours
'Fo' my stomach and soul 'll agree —
Oh, yas — yas — Honey! Byelo-o-o —

Singing

" You li'l' Lady, bye, — lo-bye —
Shet yo' li'l' sleepy eye,
Mammy gwine fetch you a dream by-m-by —
Way fum de moon dat float so high.
Mammy gwine fetch you a nice li'l' dream —
De way things are and de way dey seem —
   Bye, my pretty li'l' baby, you,
     Sleepin' sof'ly now, fer true —
      Hush — 'sh — 's-h-h —

" Eh? Whar was I? I thought I was gone —
Sho' my ears caught de plenteous sound,
De rollin' of Jorden's deep waters,
Cross which my soul is bound —
Nummine, my Honey, yo' Mammy 'll
Wait fer you right clost to de Gate —

She' ll stay dar waitin', li'l' Missy,
Nummine ef hit do be late.
And I 'll ax de Good Lord : ' Please, Sah ! Massa !
Des give *my* li'l' Missy a seat,
And some nice li'l' gol'en slippers,' —
Fit yo' neat li'l' feet ;
And a gol'en crown fer you, Lady !
Ef *I* ax him he 'll fix you up right —
Dough you is — Mammy's li'l' Lady —
Dough you is — only — des white."

De Sight of Unc' Sol

US all had done met at St. Abel's Church
　　To bury Unc' Solomon Ring,
His folks done holler, and moan, and fell out,
And done mos' ev'ything,
'Case Uncle Sol was a mighty ole man —
He said two hund'ard and two : —
He was a chunk of a boy when de stars all fell
Hoein' his row fer true.
Dey laid him out in a mighty fine coat,
Folks said 't was ole Massa's Gran'pa's
Den dey done had us all at Meetin' ag'in
To hear how his funeral was.
Us thought us done heard de las' of Unc' Sol
When de big Spring 'Vival come ;
Lord, de way dat Preacher open wid pray'r
Was 'nough to give tongue to de dumb.
But ev'ything 'peared to fall sorter flat, —
De folks wa'n't easy to 'cite ;
Us feared de 'Stracted Meetin' 'ud fail
Dat ve'y fust Wilderness Night.
But des as things was de mo'es' dull

Up rose Unc' 'Ronymus Dan.

He cl'ar his th'oat, and he riz his hand,

And he call to dat Preacher Man:

"Brother, kin I speak onct, des onct, to de Member Band?"

"Speak up, my friend," de Preacher say. "I see de wavin'
    er trees,

But de Members look cole in de Lord's gyarden,

      And I think dat a early freeze

Must 'a' cotch and nip de whole fruit-crap

      Upon dese same cole trees."

"I was off on a vigil las' night," says ole Dan;

"And my vigil swept fur and wide,

I had a mighty high wall to climb,

Wid heaven on t' o'her side.

De wall was straight, and de wall was slick,

An de wall was very tall —"

Here some of de members dey riz a groan

Which de Preacher ain't brung at all.

"Dar was nairy a notch, nor nairy a crotch

In de whole er de height er de wall,

But I hung half-way, — an' de fire — Sisters!

Was des beneath!" "O Brer, don't fall!"

"So I clumb by de eens of my fingers and toes,

Crawlin' up like a young 'possum do —"

"Um-hum!" "Good truf!" "Go up, Brer Dan!"

104

" *HE sat right side of de 'lasses pool —* "

De members was warmin' fer true.
" So, scratchin' and climbin', I retched de top !
Den ! Sisters ! De view inside ! "
(Um-hum !)
" De past'er fiel's dey was green and was wide,"
(Um-hum !)
" And I seed Uncle Solomon Ring,"
(Um-hum !)
" He had de bes' seat dat heaven could bring ! "
(Um-hum !)
" He sat by de side of de 'lasses-pool — "
(My Lord !)
" 'Lasses made by de ve'y bes' ole time rule — "
(Hey-yeh !)
" And rollin' wide in a rich, sweet pool — "
(Um-hum !)
" De pool was rich and sweet and wide —
And de pretties' Fritter-Tree grew beside — "
(Dar !)
" Uncle Sol sat under dat Fritter Tree,
Whar fritters hung thick as leaves do be ;
When he hongry he des hatter retch up, I see,
And grab a good handful offer dat tree
And eat as commojious as 'mojious could be,
Des dippin' dem fritters right into dat pool

And soppin' and eatin' away in de cool! "

(Um-hum!)

Oh, den, sah! dat Preacher he snatch up dat word,
And fer groanin' and moanin' he scurce could be heard,
He 'zorted de members to try fer dat seat —
And he 'low in all heaven hit couldn't be beat,

De seat of Unc' Solomon Ring!

'T was de bigges' Meetin' dat ever has been;
Dat Preacher he pitched into ole Father Sin!
'T was de 'Stractedest Meetin' us ever is had,
Three weeks us riz good, and trompled on bad.

All 'count of Unc' Solomon Ring!

At las' de' Vancin' Men come fum de town and said
Dat Meetin' obleeged to stop!
'Caze if niggers kept singin' and 'zortin' all night
How is dey gwine raise any crop?
Dey say ef Saint Abel dat Meetin' didn't drop,
Dey say meat-advances sho'ly would stop,
And all de meal-bags 'ud git empty and flop,
'Longer Unc' Solomon Ring —
Us hatter quit singin' and 'zortin' fer sho' —
But you know dat made niggers long all de mo'
Fer Unc' Solomon's ledjurely, heavenly sto' —
And dat blessed land whar de Fritter Tree grow,

Fer ole Unc' Solomon Ring.

*D*ARK *are the churches that dot the Black Belt,*
Dark with the painting of weather and time.

Hymns Of The Black Belt

DARK are the churches that dot the Black Belt,
Dark with the painting of weather and time;
Clumsily built of heaviest hewn logs
Grown long ago in the rich Southern clime.

Not here are columns of marble or stone,
Brush-wood tent here is the quaint portico;
No chime of bells here summon the worshipper
Only the beat of the Sweep, — clear and slow.

Yet these dark churches enfold a fair jewel
That to the Dark Race shall ever belong;
Appanage savage and slave-days bequeathed them
Treasure of wild, sweet, exuberant song.

Songs that they sing at their " Wilderness Feas',"
" Moans " that to " Moves " of the " Members " ring
true,
Chants for the weird rite of " Feedin' de Sheep,"
Wild hymns of joy when " De Seekers come th'oo."

PLANTATION SONGS

"Ballets" to time with their joyous "Hand Clappin',"
"Lead Songs," and "Follers," and "Spirituelles."
Ah! — from the dimness of dusky old churches
Rich, clear, and loud, the melody swells.

HYMN OF THE DEAD

O SOMEBODY dead in the graveyard,
And somebody dead in the sea —
Gwine to wake up and shout in de mornin',
And sing dat jubilee!
Roll, Jorden, roll —
Sister, you oughter been dar
To hear dat river roll;
You oughter been shout in de Kingdom
To hear dat water roll.

O father dat's kilt wid a bullet,
And brother dat's cyarved wid a knife
Yo' woun' 'll be heal some mornin'
When you git ter de Land of Life —
Roll, Jorden, roll!
Dar's nairy a tow nor tug-boat
To cross dat river's roll,
I wanter go 'crost in a calm time
For Jorden's chilly and cole.

O chillen dat's burnt in de cabins
Whilst dere mammies air out in de fiel',
And chillen dat hears de Death-Call
Whilst dey be dancin' a reel —
Roll, Jorden, roll!
On Jorden's bank dey 'll stan'
To hear dat water roll!
Better aim now fer Canaan's lan',
O chillen, fer Canaan's lan.'

O sister, dat's swingin' wid a fever,
And sister dat's trimblin' wid a chill,
Gwine be a Love-Feas' to-morrer,
You better had drink yo' fill:
Roll, Jorden, roll —
Dar's nairy a skiff for de sinner
To 'scape dat water's roll,
Nairy a boat nor dug-out
To save a sinner's soul.

O dem what's pizen wid conjure,
And dem dat's bit by a snake,
Dar's comin' a time to-morrer
For you to turn over and wake.
Roll, Jorden, roll!

Brother, you hatter wade in.
When you retch dat water's roll
You leave yer body's laden
Des on dis t' o'her sho'.

O mammy dat drag at de plow-handle,
And mammy dat drap at de hoe,
When you walk up de ladder to heaven
You won't hatter work no mo' —
Roll, Jorden, roll!
Mammy, go over dry shod.
When you hear dem waters roll —
Oh, you 'll sho'ly go shoutin' to Glory
Across dat river's roll.

SINGIN' ON BETHLEHEM ROAD

OPEN dem do's and let me in —
Free from my sorrer and free from my sin!
I am a-gwine to Bethlehem,
Gwine to meet Marse Canaan and Shem,
Gwine to fit on de shoes of John,
Oh, so easy I slipped 'em on.

OH, mammy, dat drag at de plow handle,
And mammy dat drap at de hoe,
When you walk up de ladder to Glory
You won't batter work no mo'.

Gwine my road in de mornin'!
O Chillen! Dat Mornin'!
De music of dat Heavenly Band
Sound so sweet in de mornin'!

Gwine th'oo to Bethlehem
Gwine meet Moses, and Aaron, and dem —
Gwine rise up when de trumpet soun',
Gwine put on de shine-line-gown!
For I profess dat I do right,
I confess my sins in de Members' sight,
Gwine my road in de mornin'!
O Chillen! Dat Mornin'!
De singin' in dat Heavenly Land
Sound so sweet in de mornin'!

HYMN OF REPENTANCE

IF I was in de ball-room when de Bridegroom come,
    If I was in de ball-room when He come!
My feet would grow so weary and my heart begin to sink,
  For de worl' would be only des hangin' on de brink,
If I was in de ball-room when He come!

PLANTATION SONGS

If I was in de ball-room when de Bridegroom come,
  If I was in de ball-room when He come!
If my banjo was a-talkin' when de worl' begin to quake,
  If my banjo was a-talkin' den my soul 'd 'gin to shake,
If my banjo was a-talkin' when He come!

If I was in de ball-room when de Bridegroom come,
  If I was in de ball-room when He come!
If my seekin' had not found, if my soul was not unbound!
  If my feet was not planted on de solid ground!
Oh, I want ter be fixed when He come —
            Hallelujah! —
              Yas —
                Yas —
                  Yas.

SONG OF THE LITTLE CHILDREN

LITTLE children, I believe!
  Been long time waggin' wid de cross,
Been long time shakin' wid de fros',
Been long time lingerin' and los' —
But now, little children, I believe!
Then now, little children, don't yer grieve.

Little children, I believe !
My heart 's done bud and bloom,
My body is ready for de tomb,
My soul kin pass th'oo de gloom,
For now, little children I believe !
My soul de good news done receive !

Little children, I believe !
My golden shoes are on my feet,
My starry crown fit so neat,
My tongue is chuned to sing so sweet —
Fer now, little children, I believe !
And my soul's white robe is weave !

WARNIN' HYMN

STARS and de elements a-fallin',
 De moon in blood drips away :
Yonder 's de Angel a-callin'
De sheep in de fold dis day !
　　Sinner ! Sinner ! Whar will yer stand
　　When de rocks begin to melt,
　　And de earth begin to shake,
　　And dar ain't no solid land ?

When de rocks begin to melt,
And de stars air swept away,
And de hail begins to pelt
And de sinner cannot pray —
    Oh, den, Hypocrit, whar will you stand
    When de trees begin to cry,
    And de hills begin to quake,
    And de solid earth 's quicksand,—

When de trees begin to cry,
And de limbs begin to swink
And de leaves dey fall to nothin'
'Caze de earth is des a brink?
    Oh, den, Seeker-man, whar will you stand
    When de sheep is on de right
    And de goats is on de left
    And dey 'll never run no mo' in a band?

When de sheep is on de right
And de goats is on de left
And dey 'll never run together any mo',
Fer de Seeker 's found a cleft —
    But de Sinner! Sinner! De Sinner 's rockin' loose
    And de Mourner 's got a seat,
    And de Member 's got a crown,
    But de Hypocrit 's rockin' loose.

SONG OF THE STORM

I WONDER what de thunder grumblin' about :
Hit chain to a cloud and can't git out ;
I wonder what de lightenin' gwine to do —
Slashin' out a hole and try ter git th'oo :
    O my soul ! Try to be bole —
    You gotter hear how Jorden roll !

I wonder why de winds air rollin' roun' :
Dey roll high up and dey roll low down —
I wonder why de waters rush and roar ;
Is dey retchin' fer de Ark and good ole Noah?
    O my soul ! Try to be bole —
    For you 'bleeged to hear how Jorden roll !

I wonder what de wile trees weepin' for,
Bendin' to de Souf and bendin' to de Nor' :
Is dey cryin' 'caze de storm do strip dey leaves
'Stroyin' all de work dat de Summer weaves —
    O my soul ! Try to be bole —
    You can't get outer hearin' how Jorden roll !

I wonder why de rains air sweepin' so :
Dey sweepin' out a place fer de new rainbow,

I wonder why de sunshine 's a-creepin' about :
Oh, des 'caze de storm is mos' wo' out —
    O my soul ! You will be bole
    For dar 's al'a's dry land fer de Member's soul.

A MEETIN' CHANT

Y OU, Hypocrit !
    You, Belzebug !
You dwellin' 'mong-a de swine,
You go 'long to Glory wid yo' tongue in yer teef
And you leave-a yo' hearts-a behine !
    Holy Warrior ! Holy Warrior !
Come to tell you ! Come to tell you !
    You better start *up* de incline.

    O Mourner, hark !
    O Sinner, turn !
Sech a lumberin' in-a de West !
Oh, a Reason come along, and he 'low to me :
Dis ain't no time-a for to rest !
    Holy Warrior ! Holy Warrior !
Come to tell you ! Come to tell you !
    Dat de narrer way is de best.

Let yo' gun be prime!
Let yo' sword be fine!
And you 'll start out to fight de devil.
You 'll find him-a ready and-a waitin' sho —
He mo' 'n apt meet you wid a shevil!
Holy Warrior! Holy Warrior!
Come to tell you! Come to tell you!
Dat de road to hell is level.

WHO BUILT THE ARK?

WHO built de ark?
Norah! Norah!
Who built de ark?
Norah! Oh,
Norah built de Ark on de highest hill.
O Sinner-man! Whar you gwine buil'?

Who 'lec' de beas'?
Norah! Norah!
Who kept de peace?
Norah! Oh,
Norah built de Ark on de dryes' lan' —
And de Sinner he 'low: " What a foolish man!"

Who snare de birds?
Norah! Norah!
Who druve de herds?
Norah! Oh,
Water in de Eas'! Water in de Wes'!
Water make de worl' a Wilderness!

Who cotch de snakes?
Norah! Norah!
In de cane-brakes —
Norah! Oh,
Norah receive de rainbow sign:
No mo' water, but fire nex' time.

SONG OF THE SEEKER

SOMETIMES I'm up; sometimes I'm down;
Trouble done bore me down —
But faith is sure, and faith is sound,
And to de Land of faith I'm bound:
Wake up, Jacob!
Wake up, John!
Sinner-man, don't you
Sleep too long.

HYMNS OF THE BLACK BELT

De hill of doubt is hard to climb,
But all de years is full of time,
And truth 's de traces tight and prime
To pull us out de mud and slime:
Wake up, Member!
Wake up, All!
Sinner-man, don't you
Hear de call?

De Member's chariot is four-wheel:
Wheel, 'Pentance hit will never creel,
Wheels, Prayer and Praise 'll never yiel',
Wheels, Pleadin' Terms is strong to feel.
Chariot strong,
Chariot long
Sinner-man, come! — whar
You belong.

Ef Hope and Love together 'll hol',
Dey 'll make a strong breas'-yoke and pole,
To pull 'long to'ard de streets of gole,
Char'ty 's de reins — pull on 'em bole:
Come den. Git in!
Git in, now!
Sinner-man, you bes'
Be quick, I 'low.

125

A SPIRITUELLE

SOMETIMES I 'm up; sometimes I 'm down —
 Almost level wid de solid groun':
For I think I hear de wheel of time,
Dat 's hot wid sand and cole wid rime —
  All round my bed a-turnin',
  All round me daylight 's burnin'.
All round my bed I hear dem angels singin';
All round my bed I hear dem charmin' bells a-ringin'.
   Sing, angels, sing!
   Ring, bells, ring!
  Don't I hear dem bells a-ringin'?

  Oh, let me get on de bright star-crown!
  Oh, let me lay de sinner-load down!
  For I think I hear white horses' feet
  Slippin' and slidin' on de gol'en street —
   All round my bed a-turnin',
   All round me daylight 's burnin'.
All round my bed I hear dem angels singin';
All round my bed I hear dem charmin' bells a-ringin'.
   Sing, angels, sing!
   Ring, bells, ring!
  Yas, I hear dem angels singin'!

HYMNS OF THE BLACK BELT

A HYMN CHUNE

OH, two white hosses standin' side and side,
    Me and Massa Gab'iel gwine for to ride!
        Hallelujah! Hallelujah!
        Sittin' by de side of de Lamb.

I went to de Meetin', I did n't go to stay,
But I got so happy dat I stayed all day!
        Hallelujah! Hallelujah!
        Sittin' by de side of de Lamb.

Oh, a contrite mind and a hick'ry-nut heart
Ef you want to go to Glory — why don't you start?
        Hallelujah! Hallelujah!
        Sittin' by de side of de Lamb.

Ef you go to Sister Mary's house talk about me
Ef you go to Sister Martha's house don't call my name.
        Hallelujah! Hallelujah!
        Sittin' by de side of de Lamb.

Oh, de white chillen has dere heaven down heah,
But de niggers hatter wait fer dere's up Dar!
        Hallelujah! Hallelujah!
        Sittin' by de side of de Lamb.

Oh, de golden slippers, and de gold wais'-band —
Ev'ything in Glory so golden and grand !
　　　Hallelujah ! Hallelujah !
　　　Sittin' by de side of de Lamb.

Oh, twenty-three balls round de Elders' throne
And dere heads all 's white as de marble-stone !
　　　Hallelujah ! Hallelujah !
　　　Sittin' by de side of de Lamb.

MEMBERS' HYMN

OH, when I was a sinner
　　I run my race so well
I soon come to find out I was hangin' over hell,
　　　I was hangin' over hell,
　　　I seed hit's fires well !

Oh, I was bound to go right down
Onless I turn right aroun'
Onless I put on de lily white robe and fasten on de
　　crown —
　　　And fasten on de crown —
　　　Yas, I turn so swif' aroun' !

128

I WENT to de Meetin', I did n't go to stay;
But I got so happy I stayed all day.

HYMNS OF THE BLACK BELT

Oh, de mornin' star so high !
But I 'll ride on it by-m-bye,
When I git whar I 'll no mo' die —
        Dar whar I 'll no mo' die,
        When I git dar by-m-bye !

Oh, us is left de sinner-seat;
Us stand firm on Zion's beat,
When de meetin' day come us 'll all gather roun',
        Us 'll all gather roun',
        Us 'll all have a gol'en crown.

Oh, spit de cup er damnation !
Oh, take up de cup er salvation !
Fer you don't want be found in de Open Fiel' —
        Don't want be found in de Open Fiel'
        When you cotch sound of de chariot wheel !

Oh, leave de sinner-seat now,
Oh, jine in de Members' Row,
Fer de Members' way is de best way to go —
        De ve'y best way to go —
        Is clost to de Members' Row !

PLANTATION SONGS

HYMN OF REJOICING

LOOK-a-yonder! Look-a-yonder!
Dar's all of de chillen right size and numberin'
Oh, in de Eas' sech a noise and a lumberin' —
Moses strike de rock and dey all pass under.
My Soul! dat dangerous thunder!
I'm standin'! standin'!
Standin' in de shoes of John!

Look-a-yonder! Look-a-yonder!
Dar's Pharaoh's chillen all runnin' and hollerin';
All Egypt's land is a-fleein' and a-follerin'.
Moses raised his hand and de elements thunder,
Pharaoh and his men were kivered under —
I'm standin'! standin'!
Standin' in de shoes of John!

Look-a-yonder! Look-a-yonder!
Dar's ole Satan at de gate er Torment,
And yonder's Heaven des crost and forment;
Satan reach for sinners wid a pitch-fork prong;
Gab'iel call de Members: Come along! Come along!
I'm standin'! standin'!
Standin' in de shoes of John!

HYMNS OF THE BLACK BELT

Look-a-yonder! Look-a-yonder!
Dar's de wheel er fire des whirlin' and twirlin',
And ole Satan on hit, him wheelin' and whirlin'.
Ole Satan! I hear you clankin' dat chain,
But you no need to make a grab at me again
  I 'm standin'! standin'!
 Standin' in de shoes of John!

Look-a-yonder! Look-a-yonder!
Dar's many a sinner, when de day comes nigh,
Dat 'll wish he 'd helt Heaven when Heaven was by;
For as Daniwell was safe in de lions' den
Oh, des dat safe is de Member when
  A-Standin'! Standin'!
 Standin' in de shoes of John!

WHO 'LL BE READY?

WHO 'LL be ready when de Bridegroom come?
 Who 'll be happy and who 'll be glum?
Jorden river so chilly and cole,
Oh, dat water so swimmin' and swole!
Dem whar 'll swim it is obleeged to swum
Des a-fo' de Angel 'll beat on de drum!
Yas! O my Soul! Dem waters roll —
  Who 'll be ready?

133

Who 'll be ready when de song 's begun ?
Who 'll be singin' and who 'll be dumb ?
Oh, dem Members a-wearin' of gole
Safe acrost de shaller and safe acrost de shoal,
Whar de gracious tree grows free and firm,
Whar de blessed welcome rises from,
For de righteous few and de righteous some.
Yas ! O my Soul ! Dem bells do toll —
      Who 'll be ready ?

Who 'll be ready when de body's numb ?
Who 'll be shoutin' and who 'll be mum ?
Oh, de Member he 'll be bole
And de Seeker will take good hol' —
      Dey 'll be ready !

HYMN OF THE WINDS

DAR 'S war in de worl', O my brothers,
    For hear how dem brief winds arise ;
Yas. De winds lift dey voice, my brothers,
Wid de breaf er dem what dies !
      Roll, winds, roll,
    And rock de Death-river's tide.
      Roll, winds, roll,
    Dat river is long and wide.

Dar 's many a soul passin' on, sisters,
For watch how dem white clouds pass by ;
Dar 's many a soul passes, sisters,
When de clouds slip fast and high.
  Roll, winds, roll,
   And rock de Death-river's tide.
  Roll, winds, roll,
  Dat river is deep and wide.

Dar 's war in de worl', O Elders,
 Brief reverend winds arise !
Dar 's war in de worl', O Elders
 And dar 's tears in de worl's eyes —
  Roll, winds, roll,
   And rock de Death-river's tide.
  Roll, winds, roll,
  Dat river is heavy and wide.

SONG OF THE SEA

DE Lord He hardened Pharaoh's heart
 Because he would not bow ;
His heart was hard as hick'ry wood
 Pitched and tarred, I 'low !

De Lord did harden Pharaoh's heart —
   Ole Pharaoh got a los' den !
Oh, watch him how he led his host
   And tried to git across den !

De Lord made good ole Moses' heart
   Des as sof' as wax is —
I 'low dat Mercy 's in it fas',
   Tight as new wove flax is !

De Lord made Moses meek and true,
   And let him come across ;
Let him smote his rod and pass along
   And would not let him git los' !

      Come across !
      Come across !
Come across, Moses, now !
  Moses' knee was soon to bow.
      Den come across !
      Den come across !
    Dar ain't no danger gittin' los' —
      Gittin' los',
      Gittin' los'.
Dar ain't no danger gittin' los' den,
When de waters roll back — how and when,
And left dry land for de Member-men.

THE WORLD'S HYMN

The Plantation Dies Iræ, Dies Illa

OH, in dat awful day
    De moon in blood 'll drip away,
Wile winds will arise,
Rise wid breaf of all dat dies.

What will de Sinner-man do dat Day?
He will go to his home to be driven away —
        Driven away !
        Driven away !

Skies gittin' grey wid gloom :
John takes his shinin' broom —
John sweeps hit far and nigh,
Sweeps de stars from out de sky.

What will de Elder-man do dat Day?
He will go to his home and dey 'll ax him to stay —
        Ax him to stay !
        Ax him to stay !

In dat one hour Day
Oceans 'll bile away;
Birds 'll forgit to fly
All livin' 'bleeged to die.

137

PLANTATION SONGS

What will de Hypocrit do dat Day?
He will knock at de do' and be driven away —
    Driven away !
    Driven away !

    Dat Day what 'll light de sky ?
    De sun 'll rise des one hour high,
    Den down dat sun will fall —
    Come in, Seekers !   Come in all !

What will de Church-Leader do dat Day ?
He will tap at de do' and dey 'll ax him to stay —
    Ax him to stay !
    Ax him to stay !

    Den when de Archangel sing
    He 'll hide his face behin' his wing ;
    Prayers 'll roll from sho' to sho'
    And Praise 'll rise ter set no mo'.

Sinner and Hypocrit *'fo'* dat Day,
Can't you come in and plead to stay —
    Plead to stay ?
    Plead to stay ?

HYMNS OF THE BLACK BELT

HYMN OF SAFETY

TALLES' tree in Paradise,
 Members call it Tree of Life —
Safe from sorrer and from strife,
Safe from sin, and safe fer Life !

Satan sought my sorrer out,
Knocked my soul around about ;
Satan aimed a ball at me,
Hit my sin, but I went free !

If a Hypocrit is nigh me,
Des don't let him spy me !
And why not Satan, too —
If he don't aim too true ?

My soul 's as light as leaven is
I 'm risin' up whar heaven is.
I knock at de gate, I do ;
I will knock twel dey let me th'oo !

HYMN OF FREEDOM

OH, de elements open
        And de love come down
Shine so bright, shine all aroun' !
I 'll out from Egypt on de furder shore,
I 'll out from Egypt, and I 'll 'turn no more !
Oh, rock-a my soul in de weary lan' —
Moses say Pharaoh's a mighty bad man !

O you, Chillen of Is'iael,
Does you un'erstan'
How Moses kilt a Egypchan
And buried dat man in Egypt lan'
Diggin' a hole in Egypt san' ? —
Oh, rock-a my soul in de weary lan' ;
Dat 's what he done to de Egypt man !

Oh, rough rocky road
I mos' done trabblin'.
Hypocrit, stop yo' tell-tale babblin' ;
I 'm tired er trabblin' in de Wilderness —
Rain in de mornin', in de evenin' res'.
Oh, rock-a my soul in de weary lan'
De trumpet is sound !   And de march is began !

HYMNS OF THE BLACK BELT

Carry my soul up yonder !

Carry my soul up yonder !

Yas ! My soul !

Um — m — m — m —

M — m — m —

M — m —

M —

THE MOURNER'S HYMN

I ACKNOLEDGE I did wrong,
I stayed in de wilderness mos' too long ;
But I 'll sign my hand to de Gospel plow,
And I 'll take my start to Glory now,
Plough dis furrough to Heaven's door,
I ain't gwine loose dis plow no more.

I acknoledge I did wrong,
But now I 'm gwine whar I belong ;
For I 'll lay my hand on de Christian hoe,
And I ain't gwine let no meanness grow —
Hoe dis row to Heaven's door,
I ain't gwine loose dis hoe no more.

141

I acknoledge I did wrong,
Onct I was singin' a banjo song;
But I 'll fill my hand wid de Gospel seed,
And I 'll sow so thick dat I 'll choke de weed —
Sow de seed to Heaven's door
I ain't gwine cease dese seed to sow.

I acknoledge I did wrong,
I stayed in de sinner-seat mos' too long;
But I 'll take my fork in harvest-time,
And I 'll fling my sins afur behine.
I 'll fork and pitch to Heaven's door,
And when I git dar I 'll work no more.
Hallelujah !

THE SOMEDAY HYMN

WHEN Abel lives again
Color 'll quit dese sons of Cain.
We 'll all be free from sorrer and pain —
In dat day ! In dat day !

When Gab'iel read dat day,
When de worl' git wrinkle' and grey,
Ef yer can't read yer name dey 'll sen' you 'way —
In dat day ! In dat day !

I ACKNOWLEDGE *I did wrong,*
I stayed in de wilderness mos' too long—

But de Member 'll read dat day
Name so plain he might and may
Find and read it out loud — and stay —
　　In dat day !　In dat day !

You better be lookin' fer dat day,
Close in de narrer-road you stay,
Den you 'll be safe — an' de y'other folks may —
　　In dat day !　In dat day !

THE ENDLESS CHANT

DE big bell done rung
　　Dat bigges' big one —
De pretties' thing my sister done
Was serve de Lord when she was young —
　　Live humble !
De table is set
De Member can feas',
He need not to cease.
　　Live humble !
De big room is swept,
De big chair is kept
Ready 'ginst de Leader-man come
Come hurryin' home —
　　Live humble !

De long seam is sewed,

Come, git in de road,

Fer de bells do ring

And de Elders sing —

Live humble !

HYMN OF TIME

DIS earth is a shuttle, my brothers,
　　Around which Time's twisted and twirl
It's wropped in a many a lap, brothers,
　　Wropped round de rollin' old worl'.
　　　　Den reel me a day from de grave,
　　　　Des reel me off time to be save ;
　　　　For de thread is cut short, O brothers,
　　　　When we retch ole Jorden's wave.

Ah, dese is de laps er Time, Elders,
　　Dar's many a day in de skein —
Ah, don't let it be cut short, Elders,
　　Fer hit can't be spliced again.
　　　　Den reel me a day from de grave,
　　　　Des reel me off time to be save ;
　　　　For de thread is snap close, O Elders,
　　　　When we tetch on Jorden's wave.

146

*O*H, *come quit de Open Fiel':*
  For you're walkin' on borrowed ground.

HYMNS OF THE BLACK BELT

Oh, de sun is a spinnin'-wheel, sisters,
   Hit spins off our thread of time ;
And dat is a brittle thread, sisters,
   Hit 's longes' lengt' lies behine.
        Den reel me a day from de grave,
        Des reel me off time to be save ;
      For de thread is broke loose, O sisters,
       When we retch ole Jorden's wave.

Yas, time is a golden thread, Members
   When hit 's spun from de wheel of de sun,
And de rollin' ole sun 'll stand still, Members
   When de stint er time is done.
        Den reel me a day from de grave,
        Des reel me off time to be save ;
      For de thread 's broke loose, O Members,
       When we tetch ole Jorden's wave.

Oh, dis worl' is a bobbin, O seekers,
   Whar de threads of time are wrop
When de bobbin is full, O Seekers,
   Bobbin and cards will drop.
        Den reel me a day from de grave,
        Des reel me off time to be save ;
      For de thread is cut short, O Seekers
       When we retch ole Jorden's wave.

THE HAPPY HYMN

OH, come quit de Open Fiel':
    For you 're walkin' on borrowed ground,
You are out on a barren land,
But you 'll own de land whar you bound,
When you step in de golden sand!

You are wearin' gyarments dat 'll tear,
And yo' cloze ain't no way grand —
But a shine-line robe you 'll sholy wear
Ef you jine wid de member band!

Den come quit de Open Fiel':
Can't yer quit yer dancin' a reel!
Won't yer catch hol' de Chariot wheel?
Won't yer come wid de Seekers, and kneel
        Come! Now!
    Quit de Open Fiel' —
        Yas, my Soul, yas!
            Come! Come! Come!
    Home! Home! Home!

150

1 - 99